FREE DVD

From Stress to Success DVD from Trivium Test Prep

Dear Customer,

Thank you for purchasing from Trivium Test Prep! Whether you're looking to join the military, get into college, or advance your career, we're honored to be a part of your journey.

To show our appreciation (and to help you relieve a little of that test-prep stress), we're offering a **FREE *PTCB Essential Test Tips DVD*** by Trivium Test Prep. Our DVD includes 35 test preparation strategies that will help keep you calm and collected before and during your big exam. All we ask is that you email us your feedback and describe your experience with our product. Amazing, awful, or just so-so: we want to hear what you have to say!

To receive your **FREE *PTCB Essential Test Tips DVD***, please email us at 5star@triviumtestprep.com. Include "Free 5 Star" in the subject line and the following information in your email:

1. The title of the product you purchased.
2. Your rating from 1 – 5 (with 5 being the best).
3. Your feedback about the product, including how our materials helped you meet your goals and ways in which we can improve our products.
4. Your full name and shipping address so we can send your **FREE *PTCB Essential Test Tips DVD***.

If you have any questions or concerns please feel free to contact us directly at 5star@triviumtestprep.com. Thank you, and good luck with your studies!

---

* Please note that the free DVD is <u>not included</u> with this book. To receive the free DVD, please follow the instructions above.

PTCB FLASH CARDS BOOK 2020-2021

Exam Prep Flash Cards Review Book for the Pharmacy Technician Certification Board Examination

Copyright © 2019 by Ascencia Test Prep

ALL RIGHTS RESERVED. By purchase of this book, you have been licensed one copy for personal use only. No part of this work may be reproduced, redistributed, or used in any form or by any means without prior written permission of the publisher and copyright owner. Ascencia Test Prep; Cirrus Test Prep; Trivium Test Prep; and Accepted, Inc. are all imprints of Trivium Test Prep, LLC.

The Pharmacy Technician Certification Board was not involved in the creation or production of this product, is not in any way affiliated with Ascencia Test Prep, and does not sponsor or endorse this product. All test names (and their acronyms) are trademarks of their respective owners. This study guide is for general information only and does not claim endorsement by any third party.

INTRODUCTION

The PTCB's Pharmacy Technician Certification Exam (PTCE) is accredited by the National Commission for Certifying Agencies (NCCA). To schedule a test, you must first get authorization from the PTCB showing you have met all the pre-qualifications. The pre-qualifications are explained in the PTCB Code of Conduct shown at the end of this chapter. After you receive authorization and pay the $129 test fee, you can schedule a test online or by phone with Pearson-VUE Professional Testing Centers. When you arrive at the center, be sure to have photo identification to prove your identity. The testing center may also collect your palm vein image digitally for verification and to protect the integrity of the test. No personal items are allowed in the testing area; you will be assigned a locker to secure your items while you test. When you enter the testing area, an employee will sign you in to a computer workstation and hand you any other materials permitted only for testing purposes. You are monitored at all times while taking the test and cannot communicate with other test-takers. Any disruptive or fraudulent behavior can cause termination of testing.

The PTCE is a computer-generated multiple-choice exam that contains ninety questions. Of the ninety questions, eighty questions are scored and ten questions are unscored. There are four possible answers for each question, but only one is correct. The exam takes 2 hours. A score of 1400/1600 or better is required to pass the exam. The range of possible scores is between 1000 and 1600 and is based off of the Modified Angoff method of testing. You will officially know if you passed the test within 1 to 3 weeks after you take the exam. Within 6 weeks, you will be sent an official certificate and wallet card stating you are a certified pharmacy technician.

What Is the PTCB?

The main governing organization for the Pharmacy Technician Certification Exam (PTCE) is the **Pharmacy Technician Certification Board (PTCB)**. The PTCB was created in 1995 by leaders in both the American Society of Health Systems Pharmacists (ASHP) and the American Pharmacist Association (APA). These leaders, realizing the need for a better way to educate pharmacy technicians on the skill sets essential to their profession, created a board of advisors who initiated a testing system that assesses the knowledge and abilities needed to perform pharmacy technician work responsibilities.

By passing the PTCE, pharmacy technicians are nationally accredited and receive the title of a Certified Pharmacy Technician, or CPhT. This accreditation proves to employers that its holder's knowledge will be beneficial to their company. The skill sets tested on the exam specifically correspond to required knowledge for performing technical and production duties in the pharmacy.

What You Need to Know to Pass the PTCE

To pass the PTCE, the PTCB requires knowledge of specific subjects related to work as a pharmacy technician. The subjects and the percentage of each subject that will be on the test are listed below:

Pharmacology (13.75%): brand and generic names of pharmaceuticals, therapeutic equivalence, strength/dose, dosage forms, physical appearance, routes of administration, duration of drug therapy, drug interactions, common and severe/adverse side effects, allergies, therapeutic contraindications, dosage and indication of legend, OTC medications, herbal and dietary supplements

Pharmacy Law and Ethics (12.50%): storage, handling, and disposal of hazardous substances; hazardous substance exposure (including prevention and treatment); controlled substance transfer regulations; controlled substance documentation for receiving, ordering, returning, loss/

theft, and destruction; formula to verify the validity of DEA numbers, record keeping, documentation, and record retention; restricted drug programs and related prescription processing requirements; professional standards related to HIPAA; requirements for consultation; recalls; infection control; professional standards; reconciliation between state and federal laws; facility, equipment, and supply requirements

Medication Safety (12.50%): error prevention strategies, patient package insert and medication guide requirements, look-alike/sound-alike medications, high-alert/high-risk medications, common safety strategies, issues that require pharmacist intervention

Sterile and Non-Sterile Compounding (8.75%): infection control, handling and disposal requirements, product stability, equipment and supplies, sterile compounding process, non-sterile compounding process

Quality Assurance (7.50%): quality assurance practices and inventory control, infection control documentation, risk management guidelines and regulations, production, efficacy and customer satisfaction measures

Medication Order Entry and Fill Process (17.50%): order entry; intake, interpretation, and data entry; calculate doses required; fill process; labeling requirements; packaging requirements; dispensing process

Inventory Management (8.75%): define NDC (National Drug Code), lot numbers, expiration dates, formulary product list, ordering and receiving, storage and removal

Billing and Reimbursement (8.75%): reimbursement policy and plans, third-party resolution, third-party reimbursement, healthcare reimbursement, coordination of benefits

Information System Usage and Application (10.00%): pharmacy-related computer applications, databases, documentation management, inventory reports, override reports, diversion reports, patient adherence, risk factors, drug allergies, side effects, electronic medical records

Pharmacy Math and Calculations: dispersed throughout other subject areas including inventory, compounding, billing and reimbursement, order entry and fill process, and pharmacology

After the PTCE

After you pass the PTCE, you will receive your certification by mail. To keep your certification current, you will be required to re-certify every 2 years. Because CPhTs are expanding their roles to better support pharmacists, changes have taken place in 2015 and 2016. Since 2015, CPhTs have been required to submit pharmacy technician-specific continuing education (CE) hours. For reinstatement, pharmacy technicians must submit 20 CE hours. Of the 20 CE hours, 2 CE hours must be in pharmacy law, and 1 CE hour must be in patient safety. As of January 1, 2016, only 10 of the total 20 CE hours may be accredited by passing a college-based equivalent course with a grade of "C." Certificate holders must also pay a reinstatement fee every 2 years.

Depending on your state, you may also be required to re-register every 2 years. Registration is state specific, and it is important to check with your state board of pharmacy and/or department of health to determine the requirements for re-registration in your state. Most states require their own set of CE hours and a re-registration fee.

Due to the professional standards of working in a pharmacy, drug-related offenses and felonies as well as other disciplinary issues may cause suspension and revocation of your license and certification. Remember that you are a trusted professional and must abide by a set of ethical standards. When you become PTCB certified, you will take an oath to uphold the PTCB Code of Conduct.

Pharmacology

What are the routes of administration of IV medications?

Pharmacodynamics

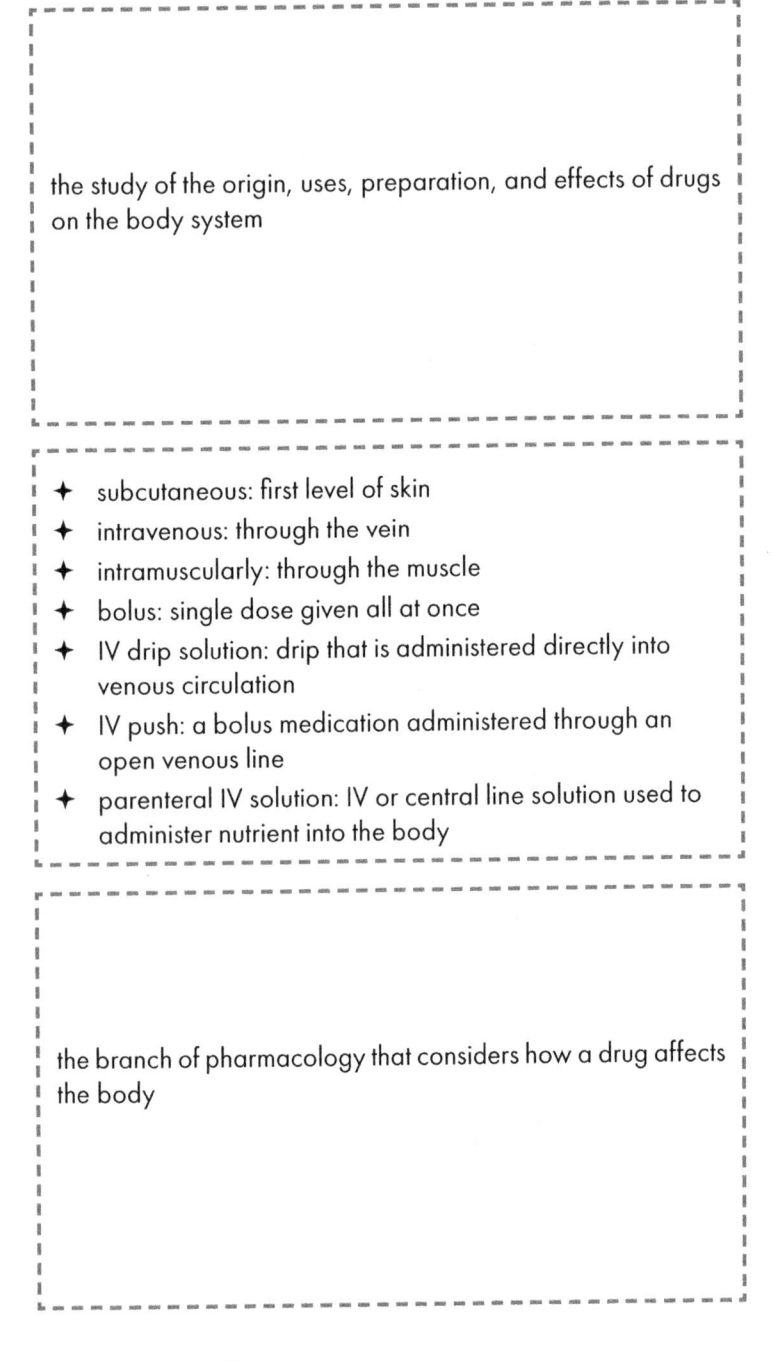

the study of the origin, uses, preparation, and effects of drugs on the body system

---

- ✦ subcutaneous: first level of skin
- ✦ intravenous: through the vein
- ✦ intramuscularly: through the muscle
- ✦ bolus: single dose given all at once
- ✦ IV drip solution: drip that is administered directly into venous circulation
- ✦ IV push: a bolus medication administered through an open venous line
- ✦ parenteral IV solution: IV or central line solution used to administer nutrient into the body

---

the branch of pharmacology that considers how a drug affects the body

What are the two ways that most drugs act on the system?

Identify and define the seven actions of drugs on the system that occur at a molecular or cellular level.

Receptor

Drugs mimic or suppress normal anatomical processes in the body; they also inhibit the growth of certain microbial or parasitic organisms.

Stimulating action: the direct effect from a receptor agonist that stimulates the body

Depressing action: the direct effects from a receptor agonist that depresses the body

Antagonizing action: the drug binding to a receptor without activating it

Stabilizing action: a drug causing a neutral reaction, neither stimulating or depressing the body

Replacing action: the accumulation of a substance in the system

Direct constructive chemical reaction: a drug producing beneficial results

Direct harmful chemical reaction: a drug causing cell destruction

---

a protein molecule in a cellular membrane that can bind to a complementary molecule

Agonist

What is a chemical that is capable of only partially activating a receptor to generate a therapeutic response?

What are the desired activities caused by the actions of drugs on the system at the molecular level and within a cellular membrane?

a chemical capable of activating a receptor to generate a therapeutic response

Partial Agonist

cellular membrane disruption; chemical reactions; and targeting and interacting with enzymes, structural proteins, transport molecules, ion channels, and ligand

What proteins are capable of producing chemical changes?

Name the molecules that carry proteins from one cellular structure to another.

What are membrane proteins called?

Enzymes

Transport Molecules

Ion Channels

What is a substance that forms a complex with a molecule, binding to a hormone, to a neurotransmitter, or to neuromodulator receptors?

Affinity

Efficacy

Ligand

the evolutionary relationship among a group of relative organisms

creating a desired result or effect for most of the population

What are some undesirable effects of drugs?

Therapeutic Window

After a therapeutic window has been established, what information is needed to determine how long the drug will be effective and to calculate the desired level of response?

harmful chemical reactions, cell mutation, multiple actions occurring at the same time, drug interaction caused by multiple drug intake, genetic conditions, and unexpected reactions

---

the quantity of a medication needed to be effective versus the quantity that would cause adverse side effects

---

Duration of action determines how long the drug will be effective by relying on the *peak concentration* of the drug. The peak concentration of the drug is dependent upon the target *plasma concentration*, or how much of the drug is present in a sample of plasma, to determine the desired level of response and efficacy of the drug.

What is the branch of pharmacology that determines what happens to a drug after it enters the body?

Bioavailability

Bioequivalent

Pharmacokinetics

---

the usable amount of the drug that reaches the body's circulation

---

This term describes a circumstance in which two drugs have the same bioavailability—they share the same chemical form and are absorbed by the body the same way—but are just formulated differently.

Identify and define the mechanisms of pharmacokinetics.

Why is the route of administration (ROA) important in regards to a drug's bioavailability?

Identify and define the different routes of administration.

Liberation: the release of a drug from its pharmaceutical formulation

Absorption: the process of a drug entering the blood

Distribution: the dispersion of the drug throughout the body's fluid and tissue

Metabolism: the transformation of a drug's compounds into drug metabolites

Excretion: the elimination of the drug from the body

The route of administration is how the drug is administered into the body. Bioavailability relies on the ROA, which means the individual drug can determine which ROA would be the most effective. Many drugs have more than one ROA, but because intravenous delivers the drug directly to the bloodstream, it usually has the quickest effect, whereas a drug taken orally usually has the longest duration. As an example, biologics must be administered intravenously because gastric acids would break down the drug too quickly and make it ineffective.

Oral (by mouth), *Sublingual* (under the tongue), *Transdermal* (through the skin), *Intramuscular* (into the muscle), *Intravenous* (into the vein), *Rectal* (into the rectum), *Vaginal* (into the vagina), *Intranasal* (through the nose), *Inhalational* (into the lungs), *Subcutaneous* (under the skin)

First-Pass Effect

Explain why pH levels can have a significant effect on drug distribution in the body.

What is the inactive transport of a biochemical substance?

when drug metabolism is greatly diminished before it is distributed into the circulatory system, due to reduction of the drug either in the liver or small intestine

---

pH levels measure acidity and alkalinity. A pH of 7 is neutral; a pH higher than 7 is more alkaline, and a pH lower than 7 is more acidic. Stomach acid is highly acidic with a pH of 1. Most drugs are weakly acidic or alkaline. When a drug is transported through the body, it encounters both acidic and basic (alkaline) environments. Depending on the individual drug, it may break down and become ineffective if improperly administered. For example, Fentanyl has a wide range of bioavailability based upon the ROA. As a lozenge, bioavailability is 50%; when used intranasally, it is 70 – 90%; however when swallowed, it is reduced to 33%. It is reduced greatly because of first-pass effect due to gastric acids.

Passive Diffusion

Because drug molecules pass over cell membranes either by a lipid pathway or water channel, this form of passive diffusion is determined based upon the concentration of water and lipids within the surface of a cell membrane.

---

the calculated volume of a drug present both in the body and in blood plasma when drug concentrations in tissues and plasma are at equilibrium

---

how proteins bind within plasma, which can affect drug efficiency and how proficiently a drug diffuses through a cell membrane

Lipid-Water Partition

Volume of Distribution

Plasma-Protein Binding

This highly permeable cell barrier makes up the walls of brain capillaries. It stops certain substances from flowing freely through the blood and entering the brain. Passage is determined by fat solubility and whether a substance's transport molecule is detectable.

What are pharmaceutical, biomedical, or behavioral research studies that include the voluntary participation of human subjects?

Identify and explain the five phases of clinical trials.

Blood-Brain Barrier

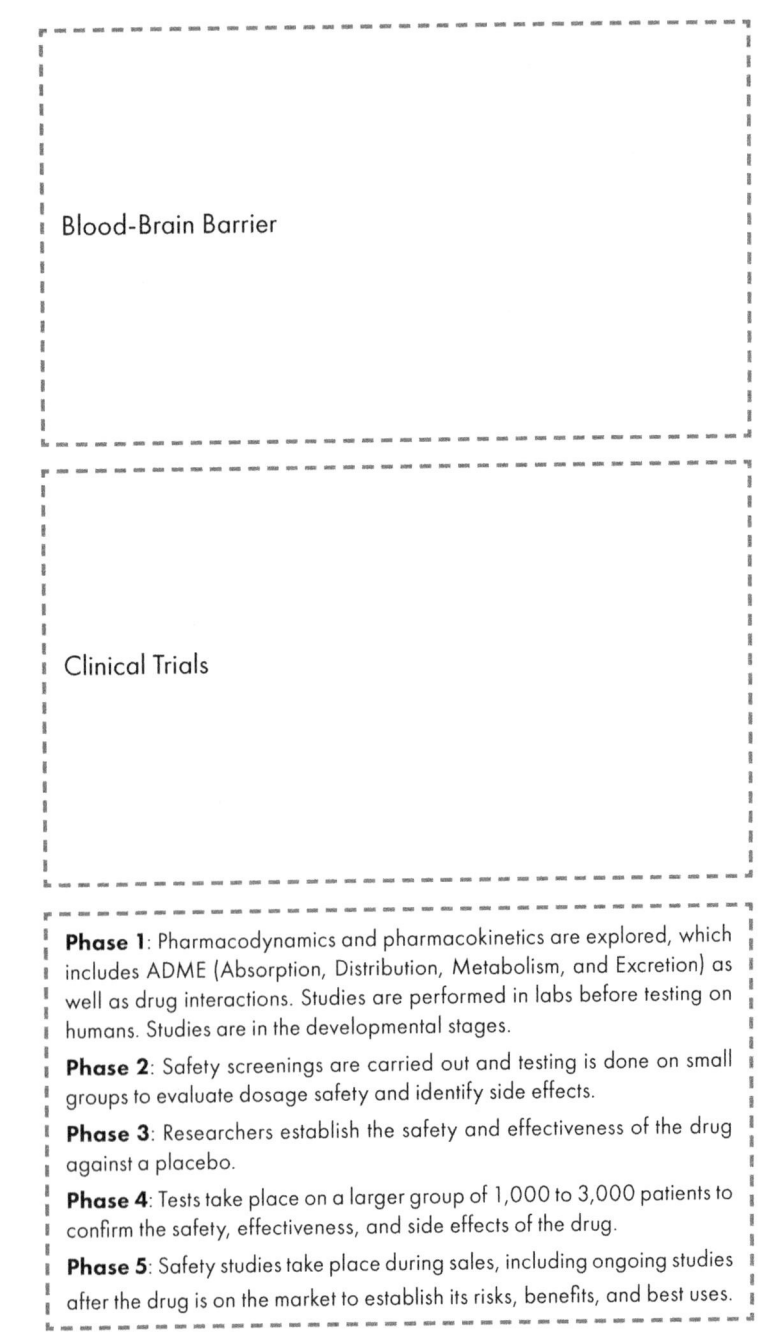

Clinical Trials

Phase 1: Pharmacodynamics and pharmacokinetics are explored, which includes ADME (Absorption, Distribution, Metabolism, and Excretion) as well as drug interactions. Studies are performed in labs before testing on humans. Studies are in the developmental stages.

Phase 2: Safety screenings are carried out and testing is done on small groups to evaluate dosage safety and identify side effects.

Phase 3: Researchers establish the safety and effectiveness of the drug against a placebo.

Phase 4: Tests take place on a larger group of 1,000 to 3,000 patients to confirm the safety, effectiveness, and side effects of the drug.

Phase 5: Safety studies take place during sales, including ongoing studies after the drug is on the market to establish its risks, benefits, and best uses.

Placebo

Dose-Response Curve

Identify and explain the three different doses that are used in the dose-response curve.

a drug that has no pharmacological effect

---

a graph which plots responses to the drug against dosage, revealing the drug's effectiveness based on the percentage of people who responded well to it

---

Effective Dose (ED50): 50 percent of the participants experience some therapeutic effect.

Toxic Dose (TD50): 50 percent of the participants experience some toxic effect.

Lethal Dose (LD50): 50 percent of the participants die.

Express *therapeutic index* quantitatively.

What does a graded dose-response curve calculate?

When investigational drugs involved in clinical trials are being conducted in a hospital, which organizations regulate the trials, what are the protocols that must be followed, and what must be documented in the logbook?

TD_{50}/ED_{50} = Therapeutic Index

Graded dose response curves calculate concentrated compounds using half maximal effective concentration (EC50) and half maximal inhibitory concentration (IC50). *EC50* refers to the concentration of the drug after a specific exposure time that activates a response halfway between the baseline and maximum dose. *IC50* measures how much of a dose is needed to activate a biochemical function.

The FDA and the Joint Commission regulate the clinical trials. Protocols cover ordering, storing, inventory, preparing, maintaining, auditing, and proper disposal of the drug. The logbook must document the drug name, strength, unit size, drug lot number, protocol titles and numbers, principal investigator, identification, date dispensed, doses dispensed, stock balance, and pharmacist's initials.

–*actone*

–*artan*

–*azosin*

This suffix refers to potassium-sparing diuretics, which increase urine flow and enhance sodium loss.

These drugs affect the cardiovascular system.

Example: spironolactone

This suffix refers to angiotensin II receptor blockers (A2RB), which block angiotensin II enzymes from specific receptor sites and help prohibit vasoconstriction.

These drugs affect the cardiovascular system.

Example: candesartan

This suffix refers to alpha-adrenergic blockers, which relax the veins and arteries so blood can easily pass through; they are antihypertensive.

These drugs affect the cardiovascular system.

Example: terazosin

–cillin

–codone

–cycline

This suffix refers to antibiotics, which inhibit the growth of or kill bacterial microorganisms.

These drugs affect the immune system.

Example: penicillin

This suffix refers to opioid painkillers, which block pain signals in the brain to provide pain relief.

These drugs affect the musculoskeletal and nervous systems.

Example: oxycodone

This suffix refers to antibiotics, which inhibit the growth of or kill bacterial microorganisms.

These drugs affect the immune system.

Example: doxycycline

–emide

–floxacin

–mycin

This suffix refers to loop diuretics, which increase urine flow and enhance sodium loss.

These drugs affect the cardiovascular system.

Example: furosemide

This suffix refers to antibiotics, which inhibit the growth of or kill bacterial microorganisms.

These drugs affect the immune system.

Example: moxifloxacin

This suffix refers to antibiotics, which inhibit the growth of or kill bacterial microorganisms.

These drugs affect the immune system.

Example: vancomycin

–olol

–olone, –osone

–pam

This suffix refers to beta-blockers (B1) or beta-adrenergic blocking agents, which block adrenaline receptors and mediate a fight-or-flight response, causing action in the heart.

These drugs affect the cardiovascular system.

Example: propranolol

This suffix refers to corticosteroids, which reduce inflammation.

These drugs affect the respiratory, immune, and musculoskeletal systems.

Example: prednisolone

This suffix refers to benzodiazepines, which reduce anxiety, relax muscles, sedate, and induce sleep.

These drugs affect the nervous system.

Example: diazepam

–pine

–pril

–razole

This suffix refers to calcium channel blockers, which relax the veins and arteries so that blood can easily pass through; they are antihypertensive.

These drugs affect the cardiovascular system.

Example: amlodipine

This suffix refers to angiotensin-converting-enzyme (ACE) inhibitors, which block the conversion of angiotensin I to angiotensin II; they may also reduce the chance of increased vasoconstriction or blood pressure.

These drugs affect the cardiovascular system.

Example: enalapril

This suffix refers to proton pump inhibitors, which inhibit the action of the gastric proton pump, reducing gastric acid production.

These drugs affect the digestive system.

Example: pantoprazole

–statin

–tidine

–vir

This suffix refers to HMG-CoA reductase inhibitors, which inhibit cholesterol production.

These drugs affect the cardiovascular system.

Example: rosuvastatin

This suffix refers to histamine-2 blockers, which reduce the amount of acid in the stomach.

These drugs affect the digestive system.

Example: ranitidine

This suffix refers to antivirals, which inhibit the growth of or kill viral microorganisms.

These drugs affect the immune system.

Example: oseltamivir

What is the name of the cavity that holds the heart, and what are the three layers of the heart wall?

What is required on DEA Form 222?

What is DEA Form 41?

The **pericardial cavity** holds the heart. The heart wall consists of the **epicardium** (the outermost layer); the **myocardium** (the middle layer of cardiac muscle that pumps blood, maintaining circulation); and the **endocardium** (the smooth, innermost layer of the heart that prevents the blood from sticking to the inside of the heart).

---

company name and address, order date, name of drug, order number of item, quantity of packages of the item ordered, package size of the item ordered, purchaser's (pharmacist's) signature, and pharmacist's DEA number

---

DEA Form 41 requests permission to destroy controlled substances. It includes the name of the drug; the number of packages; the pharmacy name, address and phone number; and the DEA number and signature of the DEA registrant.

What is DEA Form 106?

What cells are essential to the human immune system and consist of two classes: granular and agranular? (They also fight off viral infections and produce antibodies for fighting pathogen-induced infection.)

What transports oxygen and contains hemoglobin, which is rich in iron and proteins?

DEA Form 106 is used to report theft or loss. The form includes the pharmacy name, address, and phone number; DEA number; date of loss or theft; list of items stolen or lost; local police department information; and details about the container or labels, including a description and costs.

Leukocytes, or White Blood Cells

Erythrocytes, or Red Blood Cells

These are vital for blood clotting and are found in blood plasma, the liquid part of blood, which forms 55 percent of blood volume.

Explain the two states of action in a cardiac cycle.

What is the formula for *days' supply of inventory*?

Thrombocytes, or Platelets

In **systole**, the cardiac muscle contracts and moves blood from any given chamber; in **diastole**, the muscles relax and the chamber expands to fill with blood.

---

actual inventory × 7 days/cost of products sold in a week = days' supply of inventory

Identify the different types of good and bad cholesterol, as well as healthy levels of each.

Common side effects of these drugs include changes in urination, weakness, weight gain, lightheadedness, and fainting. Common interactions include blood pressure medications, NSAIDs, and anything containing potassium and alcohol.

Common side effects of these drugs include fatigue, cold hands, upset stomach, constipation, diarrhea, dizziness, shortness of breath, trouble sleeping, erectile dysfunction, depression, bradycardia, and hypotension/syncope. Common interactions include amiodarone, clonidine, diltiazem, fluconazole, reserpine, rifampin, verapamil, MAO inhibitors, and alcohol.

LDL stands for *low-density lipoproteins* and is considered "bad" cholesterol. LDL levels should be below 100 mg/dL.

HDL stands for *high-density lipoproteins* and is considered "good" cholesterol. HDL levels should range between 40 and 50 mg/dL for men and 50 and 60 mg/dL for women.

Total cholesterol should be below 200 mg/dL.

Triglycerides should be less than 150 mg/dL.

A2RBs such as candesartan (Atacand), irbesartan (Avapro), losartan (Cozaar), telmisartan (Micardis), and valsartan (Diovan)

---

beta blockers such as acebutolol (Sectral), atenolol (Tenormin), betaxolol (Kerlone), bisoprolol (Zebeta), carvedilol (Coreg), metoprolol (Lopressor), nadolol (Corgard), penbutolol (Levatol), pindolol (Visken), and propranolol (Inderal)

Common side effects of these drugs include dizziness, swelling of the ankles and feet, blurred vision, cough, fatigue, weight gain, and cold sweats. These drugs also commonly interact with clarithromycin, cyclosporine, diltiazem, itraconazole, ritonavir, sildenafil, tacrolimus, and alcohol.

Common side effects of these drugs include dry cough, nausea, vomiting, loss of appetite, and stomach discomfort. These drugs commonly interact with some blood pressure medicines, insulin, diabetes medications, NSAIDs, arthritis medications, aliskiren, and alcohol.

Common side effects of these drugs include diarrhea, lower back pain, tiredness, muscle cramps, headache, hoarseness, constipation, gas, heartburn, loss of appetite, and trouble sleeping. These drugs commonly interact with boceprevir, cimetidine, colchicine, cyclosporine, digoxin, niacin, rifampin, spironolactone, telaprevir, and HIV/AIDS drugs.

calcium channel blockers such as amlodipine (Norvasc), felodipine (Plendil), isradipine (Dynacirc), nicardipine (Cardene), nifedipine (Procardia), nisoldipine (Sular)

ACE inhibitors which include benazepril (Lotensin), captopril (Capoten), enalapril (Vasotec), fosinopril (Monopril), lisinopril (Zestril, Prinivil), moexipril (Univasc), quinapril (Accupril), ramipril (Altace), and trandolapril (Mavik)

HMG-CoA inhibitors such as atorvastatin (Lipitor), fluvastatin (Lescol), lovastatin (Mevacor), rosuvastatin (Crestor), and simvastatin (Zocor)

Common side effects of these drugs include headache, tiredness, dizziness, painful and prolonged erection, and alcohol. Common interactions include sildenafil, tadalafil, vardenafil, beta blockers, and diuretics.

Common side effects of these drugs include unusual bleeding, red or brown urine or stools, vomiting blood, heavy menstrual bleeding, and blood clotting problems. Common interactions include NSAIDs, antiviral drugs, steroid medications, and antidepressants.

These drugs are used for severely high blood pressure, acute decompensated heart failure, and in rare cases, low blood sugar.

alpha-adrenergic blockers such as doxazosin (Cardura), prazosin (Minipress), Tamsulosin (Flomax), and terazosin (Hytrin)

blood thinners such as clopidogrel (Plavix), enoxaparin (Lovenox), rivaroxaban (Xarelto) and warfarin (Coumadin)

vasodilators such as sodium nitroprusside (Nitropress), diazoxide (Proglycem), hydralazine (Apresoline), minoxidil (Minoxidil), and tolazoline (Priscoline)

These drugs are used for angina; common side effects include headache, dizziness, nausea, vomiting, and loss of appetite.

Common side effects of these drugs include dry mouth, muscle twitching, muscle weakness, loss of appetite, diarrhea, stomach cramps, and ringing in the ears.

What are the formulas for profit?

antiarrythmics such as digoxin (Lanoxin), digitoxin (Digitaline), isosorbide mononitrate (Imdur, Ismo, Monoket), isosorbide dinitrate (Isordil), quinidine, disopyramide (Norpace), flecainide (Tambocor), mexiletine (Mexitil), procainamide (Pronestyl, Procan, Procanbid), adenosine (Adenocard), amiodarone (Cordarone), and propafenone (Rythmol)

Diuretics such as furosemide (Lasix), hydrochlorothiazide (Microzide), spironolactone (Aldactone), and triamterene (Maxzide, Dyazide)

Gross profit refers to the sales of the pharmacy minus all the costs that are directly related to the sales.

The formula is: selling price − acquisition price = gross profit

Net profit is the gross profit minus the sum of all costs that are associated with dispensing the prescription.

The formula is: gross profit − dispensing fee = net profit

How do you calculate the selling price, based on the cost price and markup rate of the drug?

Explain the difference between sympathetic and parasympathetic drugs.

These drugs are used for seizure disorders, sleep disorders, anxiety disorders, muscle relaxants, and hypnotics. The most common interactions include alcohol, theophylline, aminophylline, clozapine, probenecid, valproate, seizure drugs, narcotic drugs, and allergy medicines.

When the drug is purchased at the cost price or average wholesale price (AWP) from the wholesaler, the pharmacy increases the price by a certain percentage, called the *markup rate*, which is the percentage between the cost price and selling price. After the price is fixed, the selling price is then calculated based upon a dispensing fee system. This is the professional fee the pharmacy charges.

The formula is: % markup × wholesaler price/100 = selling price

---

Sympathetic, or adrenergic agonists, stimulate the sympathetic nervous system. They mimic organic compounds such as dopamine, norepinephrine, and adrenaline in the body. These drugs are used for cardiac arrest, ADHD, and low blood pressure. Common drugs include dobutamine and amphetamines. *Parasympathetic*, or cholinergic drugs, stimulate the parasympathetic nervous system. Acetylcholine is the neurotransmitter of this system. Chemicals in this group are stimulated by nicotinic or muscarinic receptors. Examples of such drugs include varenicline (Chantix) and atropine.

---

benzodiazepines such as alprazolam (Xanax), clonazepam (Klonopin), lorazepam (Ativan), diazepam (Valium), estazolam (Prosom), flurazepam (Dalmane), quazepam (Doral), temazepam (Restoril), and triazolam (Halcion)

These drugs are used to treat anxiety, insomnia and seizure disorders. Common side effects include headache, nervousness, nausea, talkativeness, irritability, confusion, tremor, lack of concentration, euphoria, depression, and heart palpitations. Common interactions include alcohol, narcotic pain relievers, OTC cough and cold medicines, oral contraceptives, cimetidine, isoniazid, benzodiazepines, SSRIs, and digoxin.

These drugs are used to treat anxiety, insomnia, and seizure disorders. Common side effects include daytime drowsiness, dizziness, headaches, nausea, and dry mouth. Common interactions include imipramine, chlorpromazine, haloperidol, alcohol, SSRIs, rifampin, ketoconazole, and CNS-active medications.

These drugs treat depression, anxiety, and seasonal depressive disorders. Some common side effects include headaches, dry mouth, nausea, and drowsiness or dizziness.

barbiturates such as amobarbital (Amytal Sodium), butobarbital (Butisol Sodium), mephobarbital (Mebaral), phenobarbital, and secobarbital (Seconal)

hypnotics such as chloral hydrate (Noctec), eszopiclone (Lunesta), ramelteon (Rozerem), zaleplon (Sonata), and zolpidem (Ambien)

Antidepressants. Each group of antidepressants treats depression somewhat differently.

SSRIs such as citalopram (Celexa), fluoxetine (Prozac), paroxetine (Paxil), and sertraline (Zoloft) increase serotonin levels in the brain.

SNRIs such as desvenlafaxine (Pristiq), duloxetine (Cymbalta), mirtazapine (Remeron), and venlafaxine (Effexor) increase both serotonin and norepinephrine levels in the brain.

Bupropion (Wellbutrin and Zyban) is used for depression and to help quit smoking.

Tricyclic antidepressants, such as nortriptyline (Pamelor), amitriptyline (Elavil) and trazodone (Desyrel), are serotonin antagonist and reuptake inhibitors that also help with nerve pain.

What are the following drugs?
aripiprazole (Abilify), olanzapine (Zyprexa), quetiapine (Seroquel), risperidone (Risperdal), lithium carbonate, and haloperidol (Haldol)

These drugs are used for motion sickness, nausea, vomiting, rash, hives, itching, and other allergic reactions. Common side effects include blurred vision, drowsiness, dry mouth, headache, and constipation. Some common interactions include alcohol, narcotic pain medications, allergy medications, and tricyclic antidepressants.

Which drugs are used to help enhance cognition in patients with Alzheimer's disease, and what are their common side effects?

These are *antipsychotic drugs* used to treat disorders such as bipolar disorder, schizophrenia, and Tourette syndrome.

---

antihistamines and anticholinergics such as diphenhydramine (Benadryl), hydroxyzine (Atarax), meclizine (Antivert), promethazine (Promethegan), atropine, and scopolamine (Transderm Scop)

Donepezil (Aricept), memantine (Namenda), and galantamine (Razadyne) treat Alzheimer's diease. Common side effects include nausea, vomiting, and headaches.

Which drugs are dopamine promoters or precursors for use with patients with Parkinson's disease, and what are the common side effects of the drugs?

Which drugs are anticonvulsants used to treat seizures, nerve pain, and bipolar disorder? What are their common side effects?

Which drugs are considered antimigraine drugs, and what are their common side effects?

Ropinirole (Requip), benztropine (Cogentin), entacapone (Comtan), and rotigotine (Neupro) are dopamine precursors or promoters used to treat Parkinson's disease; common side effects include dizziness, fainting, and nausea.

Anticonvulsants include carbamazepine (Tegretol), lamotrigine (Lamictal), topiramate (Topamax), valproic acid (Valproate), and phenytoin (Dilantin). Common side effects include anxiety, restlessness, trouble sleeping, blurred vision, nausea, vomiting, dry mouth, drowsiness, and runny nose.

Antimigraine drugs include almotriptan (Axert), ergotamine (Ergomar), sumatriptan (Imitrex), and zolmitriptan (Zomig). Common side effects are muscle pain, nervousness, vomiting, diarrhea, upset stomach, irritability, and leg weakness.

What is the musculoskeletal system, and what is its function?

Explain how insurance reimbursement is calculated.

What drugs are used to treat muscle spasms, and what are their common side effects?

The musculoskeletal system consists of the muscles, bone, cartilage, joints, tendons, and ligaments; its function is movement.

Because the average wholesale price (AWP) of a drug is priced lower than its usual and customary price (U&C), insurance companies reimburse based on the AWP.

The typical reimbursement formula is 87% of AWP or 100% of the U&C (whichever is less) + a $3.50 dispensing fee.

Antispasmodic drugs, such as carisoprodol (Soma), baclofen (Lioresal), metaxalone (Skelaxin), methocarbamol (Robaxin), tizanidine (Zanaflex), and cyclobenzaprine (Flexeril), are used to treat muscle spasms. Common side effects include headache, nausea, constipation, swollen ankles, trouble sleeping, and weakness.

What drugs are corticosteroids, and what are their common side effects?

Allopurinol (Zyloprim), colchicine, and febuxostat (Uloric) treat what condition?

What drugs are considered non-steroidal anti-inflammatory drugs (NSAIDs), and what are their common side effects?

Methylprednisolone (Medrol), prednisone (Sterapred), dexamethasone (Decadron), and hydrocortisone (Solu-Cortef) are corticosteroids. Common side effects include a round, puffy, or "moon" face, increased appetite, weight gain, and upset stomach.

Gout

Celecoxib (Celebrex), diclofenac (Voltaren), etodolac (Lodine), ibuprofen (Motrin, Advil), meloxicam (Mobic), nabumetone (Relafen), Naproxen (Aleve, Naprosyn), and sulindac (Clinoril) are all NSAIDs. Common side effects include headache, ringing in the ears, upset stomach, diarrhea, constipation, and unusual bleeding.

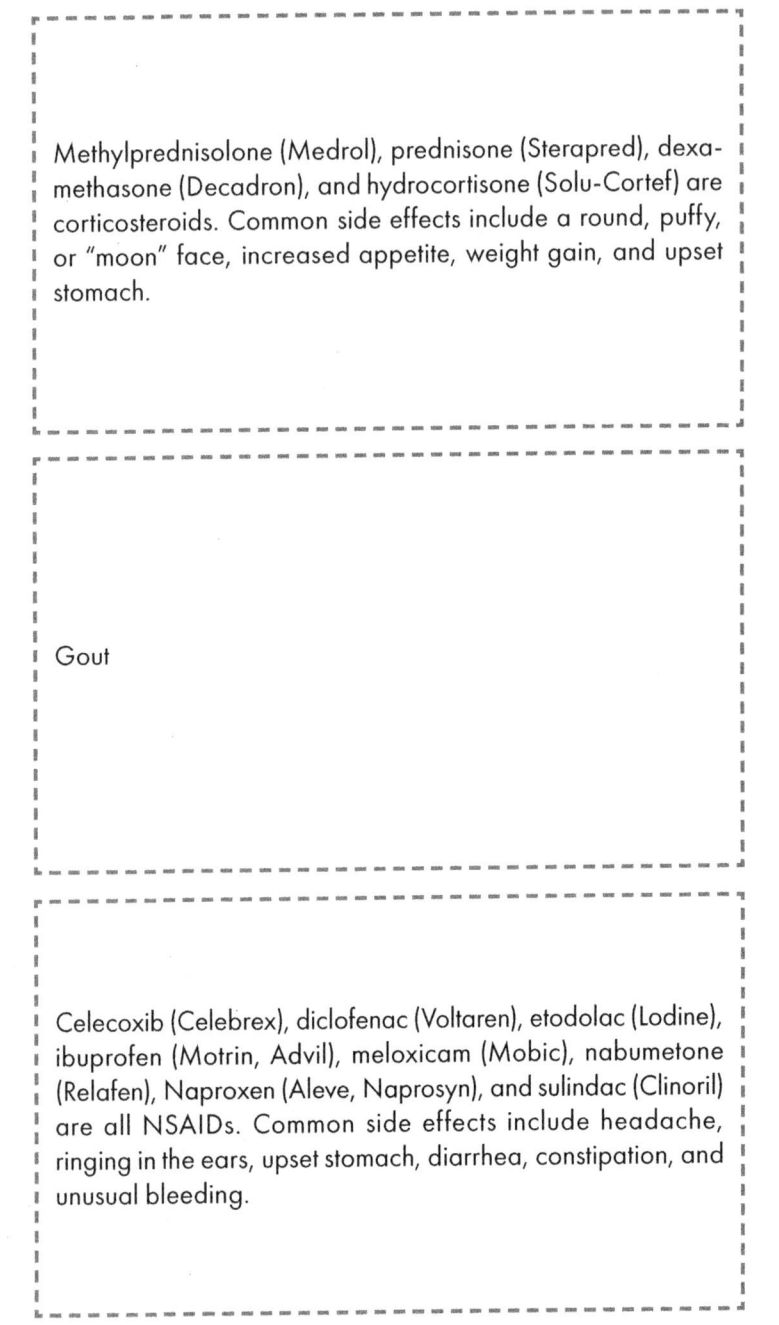

What drugs are considered opioid narcotic pain relievers, and what are their common side effects?

What drugs are considered immunosuppressants, and what are their common side effects?

What drugs are considered bone resorption inhibitors, and what are their common side effects?

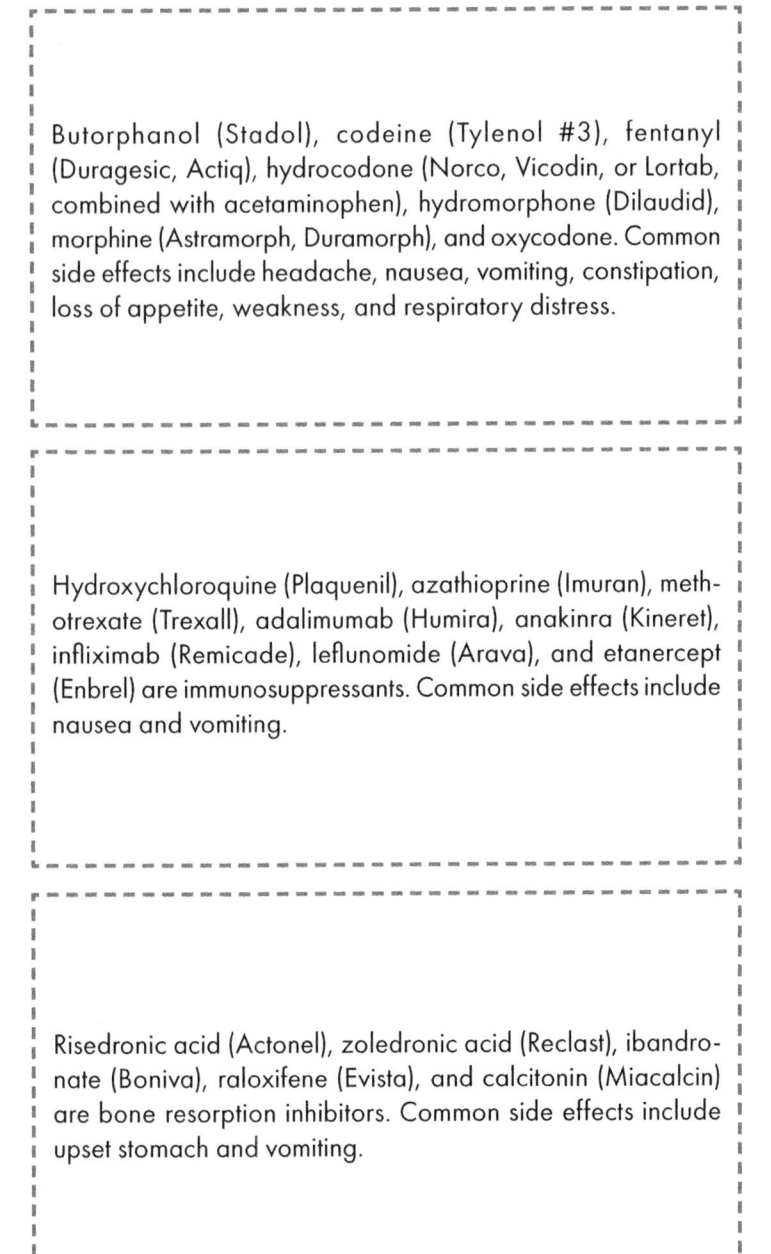

Butorphanol (Stadol), codeine (Tylenol #3), fentanyl (Duragesic, Actiq), hydrocodone (Norco, Vicodin, or Lortab, combined with acetaminophen), hydromorphone (Dilaudid), morphine (Astramorph, Duramorph), and oxycodone. Common side effects include headache, nausea, vomiting, constipation, loss of appetite, weakness, and respiratory distress.

Hydroxychloroquine (Plaquenil), azathioprine (Imuran), methotrexate (Trexall), adalimumab (Humira), anakinra (Kineret), infliximab (Remicade), leflunomide (Arava), and etanercept (Enbrel) are immunosuppressants. Common side effects include nausea and vomiting.

Risedronic acid (Actonel), zoledronic acid (Reclast), ibandronate (Boniva), raloxifene (Evista), and calcitonin (Miacalcin) are bone resorption inhibitors. Common side effects include upset stomach and vomiting.

Which drugs are considered neuromuscular blocking agents, and what are their common side effects?

Which drugs are considered histamine-2 blockers, and what are their common side effects?

What drugs are considered proton pump inhibitors, and what are their common side effects?

Pancuronium (Pavulon), rocuronium (Zemuron), succinylcholine (Quelicin), tubocurarine, benzocaine, bupivacaine (Marcaine), cocaine, lidocaine (Xylocaine, Lidoderm), and procaine (Novocain) are neuromuscular blocking agents. Common side effects include possible allergic reaction at injection site and muscle weakness and stiffness.

Cimetidine (Tagamet), famotidine (Pepcid), nizatidine (Axid), and ranitidine (Zantac) are histamine-2 blockers. Common side effects include diarrhea, dizziness, headache, and swollen breasts.

Esomeprazole (Nexium), lansoprazole (Prevacid), omeprazole (Prilosec), and pantoprazole (Protonix) are proton pump inhibitors. Common side effects include diarrhea and headache.

What drugs are considered manufactured insulin hormones, and what are their common side effects?

What are the –*ide* antidiabetics, and what are their common side effects?

What are the most common –*vir* drugs and antivirals used for HIV/AIDS and their most frequent side effects?

Insulin detemir (Levemir), insulin glargine (Lantus), insulin glulisine (Apidra), insulin isophane (Humulin/Novolin N), insulin lispro (Humalog), insulin aspart (NovoLog), insulin regular (Humulin/Novolin R), and insulin zinc (Humulin/Novolin Lente) are all manufactured insulin. Common side effects include headache, hunger, pale skin, irritability, dizziness, shakiness, and trouble concentrating.

These antidiabetics are glyburide (DiaBeta), glimepiride (Amaryl), glipizide (Glucotrol), nateglinide (Starlix), repaglinide (Prandin), dulaglutide (Trulicity), and liraglutide (Victoza). Common side effects include diarrhea, nausea, heartburn, gas, runny or stuffy nose, cough, and sneezing.

Amprenavir (Agenerase), indinavir (Crixivan), raltegravir (Isentress), ritonavir (Norvir), saquinavir (Invirase), and tipranavir (Aptivus) are protease inhibitors. Common side effects include burning sensation in arms and legs, dry and itchy skin, fatigue, increased cholesterol, increased hunger and thirst, increased urination, and skin rash. Atazanavir/cobicistat (Evotaz) is a protease inhibitor and CYP#A inhibitor; common side effects include headache, tiredness, stuffy or runny nose, weight gain and upset stomach. Lamivudine/zidovudine (Combivir) and rilpivirine (Edurant) are HIV nucleoside analog reverse transcriptase inhibitors; common side effects include headache, tiredness, stuffy or runny nose, weight gain, and upset stomach.

What are the most common –*mycin* drugs, and what are their side effects?

What are the common –*oxacin* drugs, and what are their side effects?

Pharmacy Workflow

These drugs include azithromycin (Zithromax), clarithromycin (Biaxin), and vancomycin (Vancocin). Common side effects include nausea, diarrhea, and upset stomach.

These drugs are moxifloxacin (Avelox) and levofloxacin (Levaquin). Common side effects include back pain, nausea, vomiting, diarrhea, and stomach pain.

---

the process from entering the prescription in the pharmacy software system to dispensing the prescription to the patient

What information is required on a hard copy prescription?

What does the acronym *NKA* mean?

What term describes those prescriptions a patient must take every day to treat a chronic condition?

The patient's name, phone number, and date of birth; the physician's office name, address, phone number, signature, and date; the medication strength, quantity, dose, dosage form, and route of administration; the signa or labeled directions for use; and refill information all must be on the prescription. For controlled substances, the physician's physical (not copied) signature and DEA number are required, as well as the patient's address.

No Known Allergies

---

maintenance medications

What does the acronym *DAW* mean?

What information is in a patient's profile?

This term describes drugs of the same class or that have the same function in the body.

Dispense As Written

allergy information, current medications, medical history, special considerations, and insurance information

therapeutic duplication

A drug is prescribed that has the same active ingredient as a current medication listed in the medical history of the patient. What term describes this scenario?

This is a relatively new pharmacy service resulting from the Medicare Modernization Act of 2003. Medical professionals review a patient's medical history and check for therapeutic duplications, monitor compliance in taking medications, offer patient counseling, and look out for any other inconsistencies in drug therapy.

What term describes the intermediaries between the patient and insurance company, who are contracted to collect debts and payments from the patient?

drug duplication

Medication Therapy Management

third-party payers

What is an outsourced company employed by the insurance company to manage prescription drug benefits?

In these organizations, coverage of care is limited to in-network doctors and specialists for a fixed annual fee and/or copayments for services rendered.

Formularies are lists of drugs predetermined to be covered by insurance. Identify and explain the different tiers of formulary drugs.

pharmacy benefits manager (PBM) or third-party administrator (TPA)

Health Maintenance Organizations (HMOs)

First-tier drugs are generic drugs; they have the lowest copay. Second-tier drugs are preferred brand-name drugs, with a higher copay than first-tier drugs. Third-tier drugs are non-formulary drugs; these have the highest copay.

These organizations allow patients to see any in-network physician or specialist without needing prior authorization, although they need to meet annual deductibles.

Identify and explain the different parts of Medicare.

What is Medicaid?

Preferred Provider Organizations (PPOs)

- ✦ Medicare Part A covers hospital services.
- ✦ Medicare Part B helps cover doctor's appointments and services, outpatient care, medical services, and preventive care.
- ✦ Medicare Part C covers Medicare Advantage Plans, or Medicare benefit plans covered by private health plans.
- ✦ Medicare Part D covers prescription drugs.

Medicaid is a state and federal medical assistance program for those whose income is below poverty level, blind, disabled, or members of a low income, one-parent family with dependent children.

Explain TRICARE and the three types of coverage available.

Identify the information needed from a prescription benefit card for online adjudication to bill for a prescription drug.

Online Adjudication

TRICARE is a health benefits program for active-duty military, veterans, and their families. The three types of coverage are *Standard*, which is a fee-for-service sharing plan, *Extra*, which is a PPO plan, and *Prime*, which is an HMO plan with a point-of-service (POS) option.

Cardholder's ID number and name, dependent relationship code, prescription group number, processor control number (PCN), pharmacy benefit international identification number (BIN), date of birth, and sex code are all needed.

This term refers to billing to third parties for goods and services rendered.

Reimbursement

Dispensing Fee

Identify common rejection codes that may appear on the submission screen if a claim is denied by a third-party payer.

the compensation given to the pharmacy after the collection of the patient's co-pay or deductible

a flat fee or percentage of the selling price that the pharmacy charges for professional services

These include: expired coverage, invalid patient, date of birth, person code or gender, prescribed quantity exceeds limits, refill too soon, prescriber not covered, NDC (National Drug Code) or drug not covered, and prior authorization required.

Identify common examples of health insurance fraud.

Identify the information required on a prescription label

NDC number

Common examples of health insurance fraud include billing for services not rendered, altering monetary amounts on claims, leaving information deemed important off the insurance claim, using another person's insurance card, and billing for duplicate payment.

A prescription label requires: the patient's name and address; date of prescription refill and date of most recent refill; the original prescription date and beyond-use date or expiration date; the order number; the drug manufacturer and NDC number; the name, dose, dosage strength, and quantity dispensed of the drug; the signa, or directions for use; the number of refills available; the pharmacy's name, address and phone number; the prescribing doctor's name; the initials of the pharmacist and pharmacy technician who verified and dispensed the prescription; and any auxiliary or warning labels.

---

a comprised group of numbers spaced into three groups: the labeler, product code, and package code

These are sent electronically at the time the claim is sent from the pharmacy to the third-party payer. They identify problems such as therapeutic duplications, drug duplications, disease-drug contraindications, incorrect dosages, incorrect duration of treatments, drug allergies, and drug misuse. What are they?

Identify the different information required on a medication order in institutional pharmacies.

Compounded Sterile Products (CSPs)

Drug Utilization Reviews (DURs)

The medication order requires: patient's name, drug allergies, date of birth, height, weight, and age; patient's medical condition and medical record number; patient's hospital room number and nursing unit floor; exact dosage form and strength of the drug; the drug and dosage schedule; drug preparation directions, directions for use, and route of administration.

---

sterile products that are prepared by hand in a sterile room, under sterile conditions, that are used for intravenous or sterile use; also known as IV admixtures

Central Pharmacy

What are nursing unit med rooms that have automated dispensing machines, such as AccuDose, SureMed, and Pyxis machines?

Explain how investigational drugs reach patients.

center of pharmacy operations in a hospital or healthcare facility

decentralized pharmacies

An application must be completed by a physician and approved by the FDA. Then the investigational new drug (IND) can be used in an institution following a strict protocol or through authorization by the FDA and the manufacturer by a single patient on a one-time basis. INDs require special recordkeeping and inventory management associated with the distribution of the drug to the patient.

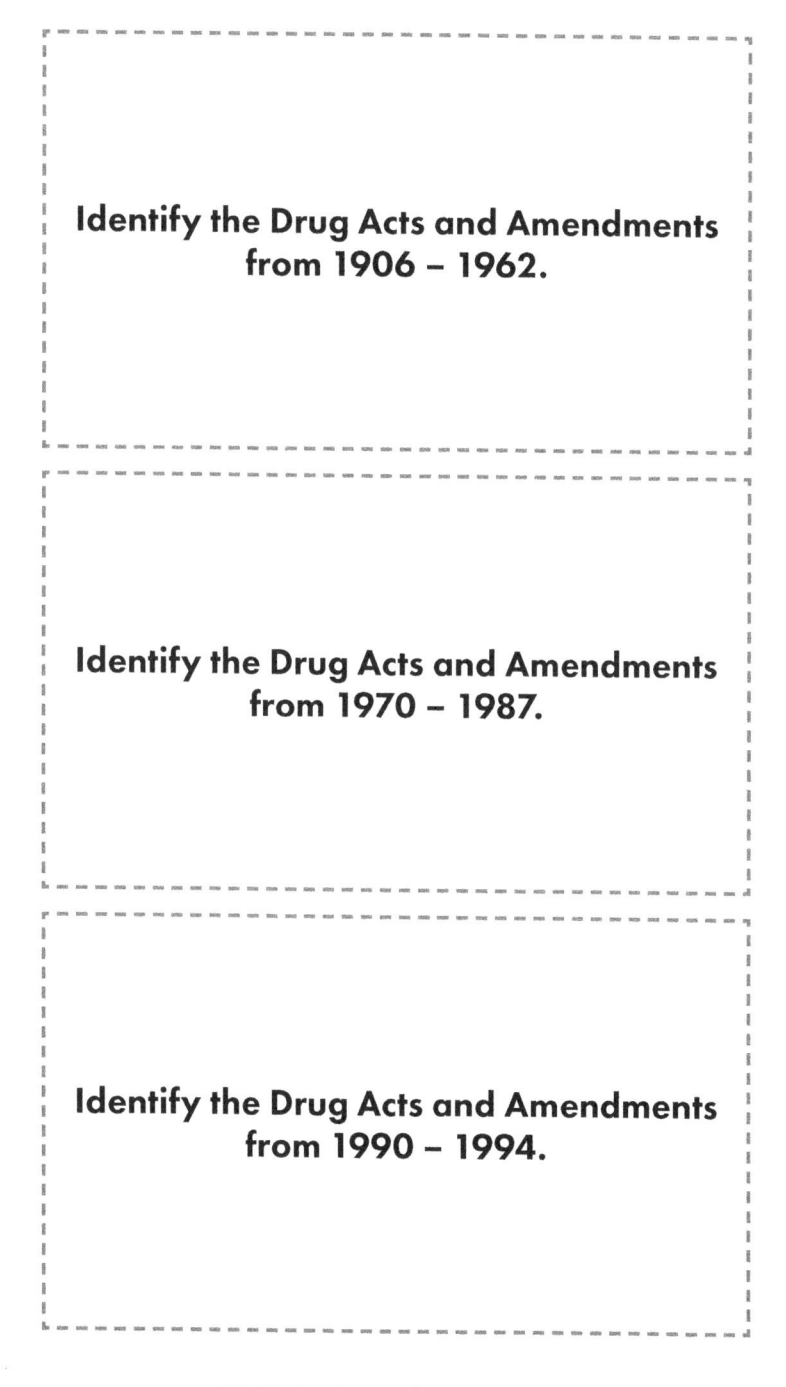

Identify the Drug Acts and Amendments from 1906 – 1962.

Identify the Drug Acts and Amendments from 1970 – 1987.

Identify the Drug Acts and Amendments from 1990 – 1994.

- Pure Food and Drug Act of 1906
- Harrison Narcotics Tax Act of 1914
- Food, Drug, and Cosmetic Act of 1938
- Durham-Humphrey Amendment of 1951
- Kefauver-Harris Amendment of 1962

- Controlled Substances Act of 1970
- Poison Prevention Packaging Act of 1970
- Drug Listing Act of 1972
- Medical Device Amendment of 1976
- Resource Conservation and Recovery Act of 1976
- Orphan Drug Act of 1983
- Drug Competition and Patent Term Restoration Act of 1984
- Prescription Drug Marketing Act of 1987

- Omnibus Reconciliation Act of 1990
- Safe Medical Devices Act of 1990
- Anabolic Steroid Act of 1990
- Dietary Health and Education Act of 1994

Explain the Health Insurance Portability and Accountability (HIPAA) Act of 1996.

Identify the Drug Acts and Amendments from 1997 – 2013.

Which agencies regulate pharmacy practice in the US?

HIPAA protects patient privacy by establishing personal health information (PHI). Healthcare workers are required to maintain patient confidentiality and keep patients' private health information, including medications, treatment, diseases, and conditions, from being disclosed without their consent. Under HIPAA, patients have the right to obtain a copy of their health information, have their healthcare information corrected, receive notices stating how their health information may be used and shared, give and rescind permission regarding how their information may be used, and receive a report stating why their information was shared.

- ✦ FDA Modernization Act of 1997
- ✦ Medicare Prescription Drug Improvement and Modernization Act of 2003
- ✦ Dietary Supplement and Nonprescription Drug Act of 2006
- ✦ Patient Protection and Affordable Care Act of 2010 (also known as Obamacare)
- ✦ Drug Quality and Security Act of 2013

- ✦ Food and Drug Administration (FDA)
- ✦ Drug Enforcement Agency (DEA)
- ✦ State Boards of Pharmacy (BOP)
- ✦ National Association of Board of Pharmacy (NABP)
- ✦ Centers for Medicare and Medicaid Services (CMS)
- ✦ Environmental Protection Agency (EPA)
- ✦ The Joint Commission
- ✦ Bureau of Alcohol, Tobacco and Firearms (ATF)

Scope of Practice

What is the Controlled Substance Act of 1970?

Identify and explain the schedules of the CSA and controlled substances.

defines whether the practitioner can diagnose or treat a condition and what prescribing authority the practitioner has

---

The CSA is a federal drug policy that strictly controls the manufacture, importation, possession, use, and distribution of certain controlled substances. The DEA and FDA oversee the CSA. The CSA implemented a scheduled class of narcotics based on abuse potential and safety. The schedules range from CI – CV.

Schedule I substances are illegal drugs that have no medical value or use. Schedule II drugs are legal drugs with medical value but that have a high potential for abuse. Schedule III drugs are legal drugs that have potential for abuse but are safer than CII drugs. Schedule IV drugs are legal drugs that have low potential for abuse and a moderate level of psychological abuse. Schedule V drugs have low potential for abuse.

How do you verify a DEA number based on the DEA formula?

What is perpetual inventory?

Explain the different filing systems used for controlled substances.

A valid number consists of two letters, six numbers, and one check digit. First, verify the first letter of the DEA number to be sure that it the correct DEA registrant type. Second, verify that the next letter is the first letter of the last name of the practitioner. Next, add the first, third, and fifth numbers of the DEA number. The last digit of the number should match the last digit of the DEA number.

Take, for example, the number AL2455562. Note that 2 + 5 + 5 = 12. Then add the second, fourth and sixth number of the DEA number and multiply by 2: 4 + 5 + 6 = 15; 15 × 2 = 30. Then add the sum of the first, third, and fifth number to the second, fourth and sixth number and multiply by 2: 12 + 30 = 42. The last digit, 2, matches the last digit of the DEA number.

Perpetual inventory is required for CII drugs. It is a handwritten log that keeps track of the ordering, inventory, dispensing, and disposal of CII narcotics. Perpetual inventory must be signed by a pharmacist and resolved every ten days by calculating the quantity balances, initialing, and adding any necessary comments.

In the **three-file system**, one file is used exclusively for CII prescriptions, another is used for CIII – CV prescriptions, and the last for non-controlled prescriptions. In the **two-file system**, one file is used only for CII prescriptions; the other is used for CIII – CV and non-controlled prescriptions. The controlled prescriptions are identified with a C stamp placed on the lower right-hand corner. In the **alternate two-file system**, all controlled prescriptions are placed in one folder. Non-controls are placed in a separate folder.

Transmitting electronic prescriptions through computer based transmission to implement error-free, accurate prescription entries is known as what?

What term describes using security features to control access to a certain resource?

What are Prescription Drug Monitoring Programs (PDMPs), and why are they significant for monitoring controlled substances?

E-prescribing

Controlled Accessibility

PDMPs are state-monitored programs that spot the possible abuse of controlled substances by identifying discrepancies in patient prescribing history, prescribers, and pharmacies in dispensing them. They deter drug abuse and support the intervention and treatment of individuals addicted to prescription drugs, supporting public health and the valid medical use of controlled substances.

Explain the Combat Methamphetamine Epidemic Act of 2005.

Medication Error

What are common drug errors?

The CMEA amends the CSA to regulate the OTC sales of ephedrine and pseudoephedrine. Patients may purchase up to 3.6 grams of these products daily every thirty days. The pharmacy is required to log every sale in a logbook and ask customers to show a photo ID and sign for the medication. Sellers must obtain certification to sell the drugs, and employees are required to receive training.

---

a healthcare action or decision that causes an unintended consequence

---

- Prescribing error: any action during the writing or dispensing of a prescription causes harm or decrease of efficacy of treatment.
- Omission errors: Prescribed dose is not administered as ordered.
- Wrong-time errors: prescribed dose is not administered at correct time.
- Unauthorized drug errors: Wrong drug is administered to patient.
- Improper dose errors: Patient receives incorrect dose than what was prescribed.
- Wrong drug preparation errors: Drug is not prepared as prescribed.
- Wrong administration techniques errors: Mistakes in the administration of the drug.
- Deteriorated drug errors: An expired drug is used or chemical potency or integrity is compromised.
- Monitoring errors: Incorrect monitoring of drugs.
- Compliance errors: Patient is not correctly complying with drug therapy.

What are the major causes of medication errors?

What are the most common high-alert medications in institutionalized settings?

To avoid confusion and errors with SALAD (look-alike/sound-alike) drugs, what strategies and requirements are used with their preparation and placement?

A patient's **physiological makeup** can cause a drug to metabolize differently than it would in other patients. **Social causes** can interfere with medication use when a patient is not under the direct care of a physician in an inpatient setting. **Calculation errors** result from miscalculating drug doses and compounding. **Abbreviation errors** can result in misinterpretations.

---

heparin, opioids, potassium chloride injections, insulin, chemotherapy agents, and neuromuscular blocking agents

---

Strategies include Tallman lettering, separating SALAD drugs from similarly named drugs, displaying written policy on precautions and procedures, defining which drugs are high risk, and annually reviewing all SALAD drugs used in the facility. Pharmacies can be proactive by storing SALAD drugs away from other drugs on the shelves, require training on precautions when using SALAD drugs, changing the appearance of SALAD drugs, applying warning labels to SALAD drugs, avoiding abbreviations when using SALAD drugs, and placing a prompt in the computer system that warns when SALAD drugs are being used.

When should expiring medication be pulled from shelves?

How can pharmacies prevent medication errors?

What should be done if an error occurs in the pharmacy?

Ninety days before the medication is to expire, the technician should mark the stock bottle. The medication must be removed thirty days before expiration.

Medication errors are prevented through multiple check systems, from prescription drop-off to pick-up; specialized computerization and automation; frequently updated policies and procedures; and education and training.

Focus on the cause and how to improve the work habits that contributed to the problem, focus on continuous quality improvements (CQI), and use methodologies such as FMEA (Failure Mode Effects Analysis) and root-cause analysis to improve quality and reduce errors.

What information is checked when researching a drug?

This written material includes data about premarket studies and prescribing information such as drug labeling, product information, pharmacology, pharmacokinetics, pharmacodynamics, clinical studies, indications, contraindications, adverse effects, warnings, drug administration, overdose precautions, supply information, preparation information, and patent information.

Explain the Occupational Safety and Health Act (OSHA) and what is required of pharmacy technicians based on its safeguards.

The Monograph: detailed written study about the drug, Chemical structure: Structural determination of the drug based on molecules and compounds. The brand or trade name: The patented name of the drug given by the manufacturer that developed it. Generic or chemical name: The name given based on its chemical makeup and not the advertised brand name. Indications: The purpose of the drug. Interactions: situations that affect drug activity. Warnings and adverse effects: Undesired or harmful effects that are the result of another drug or specific occurrence contraindicating desired drug therapy.

Package inserts

OSHA ensures safe working conditions in the United States through training, information, and education. Based on their job specification, technicians abide by specific safety guidelines. Among other things, they must observe warning labels on biohazard packaging, bandage any breaks or lesions in the skin before gloving, follow certain guidelines when handling sharps, hazardous chemicals, and infectious materials (including bodily fluids).

Material Data Safety Sheet (MSDS)

Define inventory management and what it consists of in a pharmacy setting.

PAR Levels

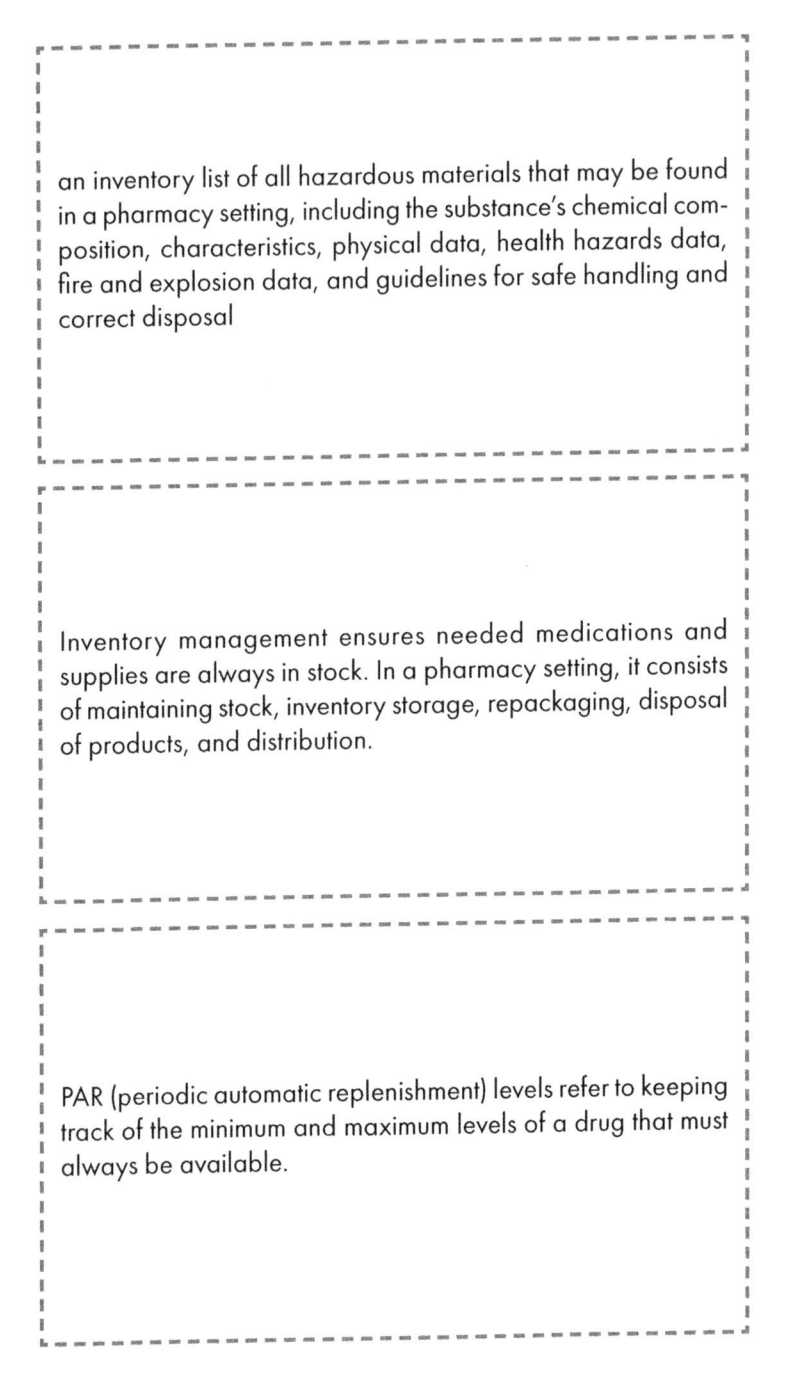

an inventory list of all hazardous materials that may be found in a pharmacy setting, including the substance's chemical composition, characteristics, physical data, health hazards data, fire and explosion data, and guidelines for safe handling and correct disposal

Inventory management ensures needed medications and supplies are always in stock. In a pharmacy setting, it consists of maintaining stock, inventory storage, repackaging, disposal of products, and distribution.

PAR (periodic automatic replenishment) levels refer to keeping track of the minimum and maximum levels of a drug that must always be available.

Name the different types of inventory systems.

Define and explain drug recalls and the differences among the three classes of recalls.

Explain drug shortages and what is required during a shortage.

- Barcode technology uses handheld scanners that scan the barcode (the NDC) on the stock bottle.
- Pareto ABC Systems use the 80/20 rule or ABC analysis to classify drugs based on their importance, value, and cost.
- Just-in-time inventory systems order drugs as demand requires.

Drug recalls are issued because the product has been determined to be harmful based on defective products, contamination, incorrect labeling, FDA interference, or improper production. In a Class I recall, use of or exposure to the product could cause an adverse event, health consequence, or death. In a Class II recall, the product may cause temporary health problems, and there is a remote possibility of an adverse health event. In a Class III recall, the product is not likely to cause an adverse event but has violated FDA regulations.

Drug shortages result when supply does not meet demand due to natural disasters, manufacturing difficulties, regulatory issues, recalls, shortages of raw materials, and changes in formulation of the product. If a drug shortage occurs, the FDA will send a notice, and the product will be placed on back order. The back order keeps the request on file with the vendor and states the date that the manufacturer believes the product will be available again. Vendors may also inform pharmacies of alternative manufacturers that have the product available for purchase and other options for supply until the product is restored.

What is drug procurement, and what are the different types used in the pharmacy practice?

What occurs after an order has been received by the pharmacy?

Explain the general stocking procedure in the pharmacy practice.

Drug procurement is the purchasing of drugs through a manufacturer, wholesaler, or a prime vendor. Different types of drug procurement include direct purchasing; wholesale purchasing (purchasing many products from one vendor source); prime vendor purchasing (a contractual relationship between a pharmacy and single wholesaler); and special ordering (used for uncommon, specific drugs needed by the pharmacy, such as cytotoxic drugs).

The first step is to verify the order by checking each individual drug and comparing the invoices and statements received with the actual product sent by the vendor. Details to be checked include the quantity, order number, and the NDC number. Next, place the stickers that accompany the order on the correct drug stock bottle; then sign and date the wholesaler's invoices and file them per policies and procedures.

Technicians should stock medications based on the manufacturer's recommendations of proper lighting, temperature, and exposure. Refrigerated items should be stocked first. Drugs are separated by route of administration. For example, stock bottles should be separated from injectable drugs, SALAD drugs, and controlled substances. Drug stock should be rotated, with earlier expiration dates placed in front; opened bottles should be marked. After drugs are separated by ROA (Route of Administration), drugs are then stocked alphabetically. Retail pharmacies stock by brand name and predominantly carry stock bottles; institutions stock by generic names and use unit dose, or blister packaging.

Non-Sterile Compounding

Explain the circumstances that would require compounding.

Per USP 795, what is required of any equipment or supplies used to compound?

the compounding of two or more ingredients that a patient can swallow, drink, insert, or apply topically; adheres to the standards of USP 795; also called *extemporaneous compounding*

Compounding is required when a product is commercially unavailable, specialized dosage strengths are needed, a product needs flavoring (usually to appeal to children), or if a different dosage form is required.

Compounding equipment must reduce ingredients to the smallest particle size, ensure the solution has no visible undiscovered matter when dispensed, and ensure uniform final distribution.

What are common products made by extemporaneous compounding?

What tools and equipment are used for extemporaneous compounding?

What is the term that describes to pulverize or reduce to a fine particle by rubbing or grinding into a powder?

ointments, creams, pastes, oil-in-water emulsions, solutions, suspensions, lotions, capsules, tablets, and suppositories

---

suppository molds, capsule filling equipment, tablet molds, compounding or ointment slabs, spatulas, blenders and mixers, balances, conical and cylindrical graduated cylinders, and mortar and pestles

---

trituration

This is required in all pharmacies and is a two-pan torsion type balance with internal and external weights. It has a capacity of 120 mg and a sensitivity of 6 mg. It must be inspected and meet the requirements of the National Bureau of Standards (NBS).

What is the required labeling on a compounded product?

What is sterile compounding?

Class A Balance

On bulk preparations, the label must include preparation name, date prepared, lot number, and amount of compounded medication. If the medication is patient specific, the label must include the patient's name, address, physician information, prescription number, and directions for use. All compounds must be logged in a compounding log with the name of the products used, lot numbers, expiration and beyond-use dates (BUD), quantity made and number of ingredients used, the initials of the technician who prepared the medication and the pharmacists who verified it, and must be filed as a permanent record.

Sterile compounding is the manipulation of a sterile or non-sterile product to create a patient specific sterile finished product for intravenous or parenteral use.

Explain the different types of microorganisms that cause infection transmission and what the technician must know to prevent microbial contamination in the clean room

---

Explain gowning up, or garbing, used in aseptic technique.

Describe the clean room setup.

Bacteria, virus and fungi can become pyrogens if introduced to the bloodstream. Technicians should be aware of their **personal surroundings**, limiting hair products and makeup, maintaining personal hygiene, avoiding jewelry, and using proper aseptic technique. They must safeguard their **environmental surroundings**, maintaining air quality in the clean room, and their **surface area surroundings**, cleaning and sterilizing tools and equipment.

Garbing takes place in the anteroom. A worker first puts on shoe covers, then the bouffant cap and mask. Aseptic hand-washing occurs next. The worker then dons the gown and enters the sterile room. Workers then re-wash hands, using alcohol-based cleanser, then don gloves over the sleeves of the gown. Beside shoe covers, garb should never touch the floor.

The clean room is free from dust and other contaminants. It consists of the anteroom, where preparation takes place and where CSP (Compounded Sterile Preparations) labeling, garbing, staging of components, order entry, and storage occur. Air quality is at least ISO 6 to ISO 8 standard, or 3,520,000 particles or less. The clean room is where the laminar airflow workbench (LAFW) is located.

Explain the difference between a horizontal and vertical LAFW (Laminar Air Flow Workbenches).

What are the air quality requirements in the sterile room, and what equipment ensures air quality?

Explain the characteristics of a syringe and needle.

Nonhazardous CSPs are prepared in a **horizontal LAFW**, which pushes positive pressure toward the preparer. A **vertical LAFW** pushes negative air pressure away from the preparer and is used for hazardous CSPs such as radiopharmaceuticals.

The sterile room permits a maximum of 3,500 airborne particles of no larger than 0.5 microns each per square meter, making it a Class A or Class 100 environment. Air is cycled at 90 to 100 feet per minute in this ISO 5 environment. HEPA filters remove all but the finest particulates, and the air is at a higher pressure than what is required for normal ventilation and comfort. Filters are checked every six months to prevent contamination by air from other rooms.

Syringes are sterile, prepackaged, non-pyrogenic, and ready to use. They are available in 1, 3, 5, 10, 20, 30, 40, and 60 mL sizes and are calibrated for measuring. The **plunger** is the movable cylinder that inserts into the barrel. The **barrel** is the part of the syringe that holds the medication and is calibrated for measuring. The **flange** is where the barrel is inserted, and the **tip** is where the needle is attached. Syringe **needles** are sterilized and individually wrapped. They draw medication from the vial and push medication into the IV bag. The **hub** is the end of the needle that attaches to the syringe. The **shaft** is the long, slender stem of the needle. The **bevel** is the sharp, pointed tip, and the **lumen** is the hollow bore of the needle shaft.

What are the most common solutions used in IV admixture preparation?

What factors can affect sterile compounding?

Explain the different risk levels of CSPs.

normal saline (salt), dextrose, Lactated Ringer's, and potassium chloride

---

chemical degradation, drug precipitation, and photo degradation

---

+ **Risk level 1** covers all medications and procedures used in compounding CSPs.
+ **Risk level 2** covers bulk compounding and all procedures covered under risk level 1.
+ **Risk Level 3** covers all requirements of level 1 and 2 as well as handling of non-sterile compounds and delayed purifications.

What are requirements of IV medication orders and labeling?

What is the formula for compounding in regards to concentration (weight in volume basis)?

What are the three formulas used to calculate concentration by percentages?

The physician uses bloodwork, disease states, other drug therapies, and weight to determine the order. Information included on IV medication order includes: the type of medication, IV fluid used, and volume needed. IV orders are given as a one-time fill or placed on a schedule. The labeling will have the infusion (dosing) rate, the flow rate (drops per minute or per hour of infusion), infusion time, and total volume needed. The pharmacist checks for incompatibilities, storage requirements, and any special instructions required. The label will be generated with patient's name, ID number, hospital room, IV solution, volume, medication, strength, and instructions. After preparation, the preparer initials and adds auxiliary labels and beyond-use date (BUD); the pharmacist verifies the order.

IV (or IW) × IS = FV (or FW) × FS

+ Weight/Weight (w/w%)
+ Volume/Volume (v/v%)
+ Weight/Volume (w/v%)

What is the formula for dilution?

What are the formulas for calculating dosage in infants and children?

What are the formulas for IV flow rates?

$C_1 V_1 = C_2 V_2$

- Clark's Rule: weight of the child/150 × average adult dose
- Young's Rule: adult dose × age/age +12
- Fried's Rule: child's age in months/150 × adult dose

Volume of IV solution/hours or volume of IV solution/minutes. To calculate how many hours the IV solution will be infused: volume in mL/rate = hours

What is the formula to calculate drop rate?

What is the drug suffix used for histamine-2 blockers?

What is the weight limit of a Class A balance?

gtts/min = full volume of solution/60 min × gtts/min of IV tubing

—tidine

120 mg

The drug *ondansetron* is used for what?

Approximately how many medication errors occur in the United States each year?

How is 2014 written in roman numerals?

nausea

1.5 million

MMXIV

The root word *lapar/o* means

What does the drug *salmeterol* do?

What chapter of the USP addresses non-sterile compounding?

abdomen

It prevents asthma attacks and bronchospasms.

795

Harvey Wiley, the chief chemist for the Bureau of Chemistry, helped to pass which act?

What is the definition of the suffix –*stomy*?

Medication errors are the _____ leading cause of preventable death and injuries in the United States.

the Pure Food and Drug Act of 1906

artificial opening

third

In which year was the Food and Drug Administration formed?

What medication error occurs when the prescribed dose is not administered as ordered?

What incident helped to pass the Food, Drug, and Cosmetic Act of 1938?

1906

omission errors

the Sulfanilamide Tragedy

What can workers do in the clean room?

The US Pharmacopeia (USP) was developed under what act?

What act or amendment required that the phrase, *Caution: Federal Law Prohibits Dispensing without a Prescription* be placed on prescription labeling?

prepare CSPs

the Food, Drug, and Cosmetic Act of 1938

the Durham-Humphrey Amendment of 1951

How often should the weights on a class A balance be calibrated?

The prefix *cirrh–* means

What act outlines the process for drug companies to file an abbreviated new drug application (ANDA)?

annually

yellow

the Drug Price Competition and Patent Term Restoration Act of 1984

How is MMMDCVI written in arabic numerals?

The suffix –*raxole* refers to what drug class?

In hospitals, how many people die annually from medication errors?

3,606

proton pump inhibitors

400,000

How many digits does an NDC number consist of?

The first five digits of the NDC number refer to what?

Medication errors that occur because of metabolism problems in patients are due to what?

ten

labeler

physiological make up

What form of hepatitis cannot spread by sexual contact?

NDC numbers were implemented under what act?

The sig code QID is defined as what?

Hepatitis A

the Drug Listing Act of 1972

four times daily

Another word for co-insurance is what?

The prefix *peri–* means what?

What medical device class of the Medical Device Amendment of 1976 referred to general controlled devices with low risks to humans?

deductible

around

Class I

Which agency has the complete authority to enforce the Resource Conservation and Recovery Act of 1976?

If a healthcare provider is unable to make an outpatient comply with directions for the use of a prescription drug, this error is due to _____.

Child doses are calculated by the child's what?

EPA (Environmental Protection Agency)

social causes

weight

About what percentage of the United States population has insurance?

What is the main purpose of MTM (Medication Therapy Management)?

Hypertension occurs when the blood pressure reading is over what?

84%

to improve patient compliance

140/90

What information is NOT found in a compounding log?

How would the instructions, "Take 2 tablets in the morning and 1 tablet in the evening as needed" be written using sig codes?

How would 5% be presented in decimals?

physician's name

Take 2 ts qam and 1 t qpm prn

0.05

Which is used for weighing non-sterile compound ingredients?

How many credit hours of continuing education on the topic of medication safety does the PTCB require to be recertified every 2 years?

Which drug typically contains an agent that resembles the disease that is being treated and causes the pathogen responsible for the disease to weaken or become destroyed in the human body?

counter balance

1

vaccinations

How long is a non-controlled prescription valid?

What does the term *osteomalacia* mean?

Which agency approves the use of investigational new drugs (INDs)?

one year from the date it is written

the softening of bone

FDA

Which sig code means dispense such doses?

What is done in Phase 3 of a clinical trial?

What is a decentralized pharmacy?

dtd

final confirmation of safety and efficacy; test a larger group of 1,000 to 3,000 to confirm safety, effectiveness, and side effects

nursing unit med rooms that contain an automated dispensing machine

When was OSHA (Occupational Safety and Health Administration) established?

Which HIPAA (Health Insurance Portability and Accountability Act) penalty tier states that the covered entity acted with willful neglect and corrected the problem within 30 days?

What is on a patient's compounding label?

1970

Tier 3

patient's social security number

What is chemical structure?

What is volume of distribution in pharmacokinetics?

The Affordable Care Act was initiated to

the structural determination of a drug based on molecules and chemical compounds

is the hypothetical amount of volume needed to administer the total supply of a drug at the same absorption rate that is observed in blood plasma

increase the quality and affordability of healthcare by helping to lower the costs of public and private insurance and lower the amount of uninsured persons in the United States

What is the most important preventive measure in infection control?

What are secondary resources?

What agency regulates the practice of pharmacy by state?

proper handwashing

---

indexing services or abstracts of publications that require a subscription

---

the BOP (Board of Pharmacy)

What agency does the National Association of Boards of Pharmacy (NABP) work with to develop and implement uniform standards relating to pharmacy?

Define *tympanoplasty* by defining the root word and suffix.

What does the prefix *para–* mean?

the BOP

---

tympano-: ear drum or tympanic membrane
-plasty: molding, formation, or surgical repair

---

near, beside

Prescribing authority was established by what?

Which organization is in charge of regulating safety in the workplace?

A red blood cell is also called what?

the Durham-Humphrey Amendment of 1951

OSHA

an erythrocyte

The drug class suffix –*pam* refers to what?

On a hard copy prescription, a prescriber has written *lorazepam 1mg, take 1 tablet by mouth at bedtime, #30* for the patient. Which would be the dose?

What amendment required the phrase *Caution: Federal Law Prohibits Dispensing without a Prescription* to be placed on all prescription labels?

benzodiazepines

tablet

the Durham-Humphrey Amendment of 1951

What is a therapeutic window?

What did the Poison Prevention Packaging Act of 1970 require?

A wrong dosage form error happens when...

a quantity of medication that is both an effective dose and an amount that avoids adverse side effects

that manufacturers and pharmacies must place all medication in containers with childproof caps or packaging

The prescribed route of administration of the drug is incorrect.

For how long is a non-controlled medication prescription viable after it is written by the physician?

What is the purpose of the State Boards of Pharmacy?

Why is it important to have the correct physician location entered on the prescription if the physician has multiple offices?

a year from the date it is written

focus on the public's health and the implementation and enforcement of state laws of the pharmacy practice

The pharmacy may need to call the physician for refills or questions. Calling the wrong office is inconvenient and wastes time.

One-half grain is equal to what?

In the word *electrocardiogram*, –*gram* is defined as what?

If a person has myasthenia, what does he or she have?

32.5 mg

to record or picture

muscle weakness

With regard to expiring medications, when are stock bottles removed from the shelf?

What describes when a prescription has no refills left and the physician's office gives more refills on the prescription?

What is equivalent to 2 ounces?

one month before expiring

a refill authorization

60 ml

Which stage of FMEA consists of identifying any failures in the process and determining why the failure is occurring?

What is the definition of leukocytopenia?

A pharmacy technician incorrectly reads a prescription label. Which multiple-check system has failed?

Stage 3

decreased number of white blood cells

dispensing

What is the definition of *triturate*?

What is the first and most important step taken when inputting new prescriptions for patients?

Which reference material identifies approved drug products and includes evaluations of therapeutic equivalents (generic drugs)?

to rub or crush into a fine powder

---

being sure to enter the correct information under the correct patient profile

---

the *Orange Book*

What compound can be made using a mold?

Wha is amniocentesis?

What is a route of administration for sterile compounding?

a tablet

a surgical procedure for collecting amniotic fluid

intravenous

In the word *epidermal*, which word part means upon, above?

Which must be first verified upon removing the bottle from the shelf when filling a prescription?

In the word *osteomyelitis*, which word part means muscle?

epi–, the prefix

the NDC number

myel, one of the word roots

Which drug tier is for preferred brand names?

Which DEA registrant type is used for a hospital or clinic?

When was the USP (United States Pharmacopeia) made a legal standard?

Tier 2

B

1907

What is a PCN (Processor Control Number) on the patient's medical ID card?

What is the WAC?

A retrospective payment is also known as what?

a number used by PBMs (Pharmacy Benefit Manager) for network benefit routing; it may change depending on what benefit is being billed

The WAC (Wholesale Acquisition Cost) is the list price for which the manufacturer sells the drug to the wholesaler.

fee-for-service

What does the systolic reading in blood pressure measure?

What are drugs with the suffix –*pril*?

the pressure as the heart pumps blood through the body

ACE inhibitors

Made in the USA
Middletown, DE
12 July 2020